Nora
Sleepszzzzz....

HB MEDIA

Copyright © 2026
Published by Habe-Burbach
All rights reserved.

ISBN 979-8-9950144-0-9 (Paperback Edition)
ISBN 979-8-9950144-1-6 (eBook Edition)
ISBN 979-8-9950144-2-3 (Limited Edition Hardcover)

Printed in the United States of America
by

Redbrush

Lincoln, Nebraska

This is Nora. Tiny and bright, learning new things every morning and night.

A busy and happy home with Mom and Dad.
Pets, toys, and giggles. Nothing feels bad.
There is a hand to hold and a lap to share. With
siblings who love her, Nora hasn't a care.

Nora is happy, no matter the place,
Loved and safe, a warm embrace.

Shhhhhhh . . . Nora sleeps.

Rolling through the aisles with her brother,
cheek-to-cheek. There is time to dream
while the wheels squeak.

Shhhhhhh . . .
Nora sleeps.

Swish, slosh, and whoosh,
the fish swim and play.
Nora blinks, slowly
slipping away.

Shhhhhhh . . .
Nora sleeps.

Such a beautiful day! Sibling skips.
On Grandpa's driveway, fun filled trips.

Shhhhhhhh . . . Nora sleeps.

Side by side on a gentle lane.
Gravel sounds like silver rain.

Shhhhhhh . . .
both children sleep.

Dresses, fins and a make-believe shore.
One mermaid yawns, then gives a real-life snore.

Shhhhhhh . . .
the little mermaid sleeps.

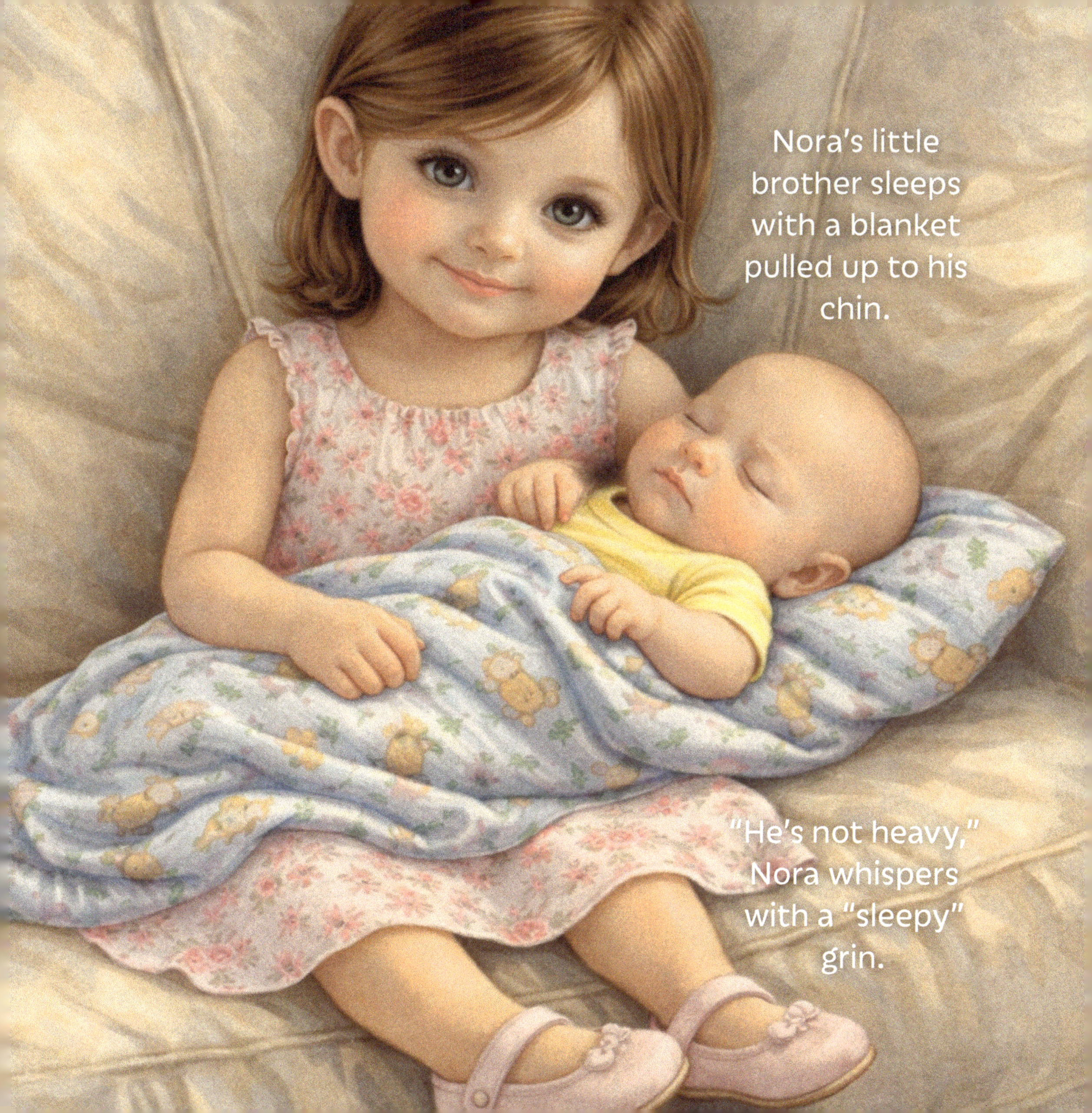

Nora's little brother sleeps with a blanket pulled up to his chin.

"He's not heavy," Nora whispers with a "sleepy" grin.

Shhhhhhh . . .
Nora sleeps.

Mom and Dad must do their work. At their screens they stare.
Nora sneaks into their office and sees the comfy chair.

Shhhhhhhh . . .
Nora sleeps.

Monkeys chatter. Flamingos sway.
They stop for a picnic along the way.

Shhhhhhh . . .
Nora sleeps.

Bedtime, bath time, and one more chore. Too tired now, right on this floor.

Shhhhhhh . . .
Nora sleeps.

Nora helps with the baby.
Mama makes the plates.
Under the table . . .
Nora sits and waits.

Shhhhhhh . . .
Nora sleeps.

Floors, chairs,
parks, and stores.
She dozes in all
those places
and more!

Night comes, soft and deep.
In her own bed is where
Nora will sleep.

Shhhhhhhh . . .
Nora sleeps.

Daddy is near, she hears him speak. Just to be sure, Nora sneaks a peek.

He is near, I know
I am safe

Children rest best when they feel secure, seen, soothed, and safe.

Gentle routines, calm spaces, and steady love teach their small bodies and brains that the world is okay, and sleep becomes a natural friend. A cuddle, a story, a soft light, and a predictable rhythm can turn any place into a safe place to drift.

Nora Sleeps is a story of a real-life healthy, energetic toddler named Nora. Nora is continually active every day with her brothers and sisters. They love to play. They love to fight. They love each other and their parents.

Nora is blessed to live in a family that is faith-filled and loving. There is safety and security as the mother and father cared deeply for their children and want them to feel safe… safe enough to fall asleep anywhere.

Nora's mom and dad remember their childhood growing up safe and secure, and are so happy to provide that same security to their children.

Nora is a bright and curious 6-year-old who loves animals, playing outside, and going on adventures with her siblings. The photos that inspired this book were taken when she was between 18 months and 3 years old, an age full of naps in the funniest places! Her silly sleeping spots brought lots of smiles to her family and are now shared in this story for others to enjoy too, a sweet reminder of childhood wonder and the beauty of ordinary moments.

About the Author

Larry Keiter is the author of a series of publications under the *Unleash Your Amazing!* heading. Larry's first book is called *Unleash Your Amazing! — Awareness Is the Gateway.* Larry shares stories of his leadership journey in corporate America and the impact of self-awareness on anyone's professional journey. This book is meant for leaders in business but can also be applied to head of households.

Nora Sleeps is a product of the same mindset that *Unleashes the Amazing* within our children. Creating awareness that providing a safe environment for children to grow and flourish will provide success for the children and family, for years to come.

"I captured these pictures of Nora napping in the middle of our crazy, chaotic life and saw them as funny moments to share with my family. Now, I see them as a testament to the safety she must have felt to fall asleep so easily anywhere. It is a heart-warming look at the quiet comfort she found right in the middle of our beautiful mess."

— Jessica "Nora's mom" Urbanovsky